Cats

one's good

two can be fun

three are a hand full

four - you're in trouble

Cats - subservient masters

I'd love cats even if I could trust them.

Ruby Sue Tootser

Tabby Kittens at Midnight

By
Christine Thomas Doran

Illustrations
Kathi Bixler

Acknowledgements

There are a few wonderful cat loving people I would like to thank in appreciation for making this book, Tabby Kittens at Midnight, magically appear before my eyes after it hid away in a file since 1999!

First, I would like to thank my husband, Tom Doran, for his patience, kindness, and encouragement in this long awaited personal pursuit.

Second, I would like to thank Kathi Bixler for the exquisite art interpretations of my text. She made each character spring to life with her colorful and whimsical illustrations.

Last, but not least, I would like to express sincere gratitude to Bob O'Brien from Prose Press who painstakingly helped in this creative endeavor with his computer wizardry.

~ Christine Thomas Doran

"Tabby Kittens at Midnight"
Copyright © 2016
Christine Thomas Doran

All rights reserved. This publication may not be reproduced, stored in a retrieval system, or transmittedin any form, recording, mechanical, electronic,or photocopy, without written permission of the author. The only exception is brief quotations used in book reviews.

Comments: flashandfancy@gmail.com

Paper Back ISBN: 978-1-941069-53-0
Hard Cover ISBN: 978-1-941069-54-7

Prose Press - Pawleys Island, SC   prosencons@live,com

Dedication

I would like to dedicate this little book to the wonderful staff at Saint Frances Animal Center in Georgetown, SC. In this truly special place, the staff provides a secure and loving environment for abandoned and neglected cats and dogs until these animals can be adopted into a nurturing and loving home environment. I would also like to give a sincere thanks to all those great people at Saint Frances Animal Center who have provided for my daughter, Heather, a workplace where she is treated with respect and appreciation.

~ Christine Thomas Doran

Tabby kittens at midnight, have slept all day,
Tasha, Toby, and Tedley are ready for a night of play.
Shhhh! The family is sleeping, so the door they'll push, pushh, pushhh.
Tiptoeing along on silver gray boots, hush, hushh hushhh!
Wait! It's Theo, peeking around the door.
"Come with us," mews Tasha, "and we'll have fun galore!
Oh, Theo! You are such a sleepy head,
You have so much trouble getting out of bed!"

Slinking, sneaking down the stairs, the kittens need no light.
"We can see so very well!" they murr* with delight.
Twitching whiskers, glowing eyes, their tails are straight and tall.
Mischievous kittens at midnight go sashaying down the hall.

*A murr is a combination of a meow and a purr.

Whirling like a tornado, things go bump, crash, boom!
"There are too many things in our way in this room!"
Rolling and wrestling, they are gymnasts in a tumble.
Leaping here and climbing there, everything's in a jumble!

Pirouetting along the mantle on her velvet ballet paws,
Graceful Tasha is a French ballerina,
"S'il vous plait!* May I have your applause?"

*"S'il vous plait" means "please" in French.

Balancing across a window sill, his paws high in the air.
Daring Tedley is a fearless tightrope walker,
"Did I give you a scare?"

Clawing up a curtain, a billowing sail to float and sway,
Dashing Toby is a swashbuckling pirate,
"Aarrrr! Watch me sail awaaay!"

Gazing in a mirror like an ancient castle's window,

Gallant Theo is a glimmering knight on horseback,

"Hark! I spy yon dragon way down below!"

Four stalking felines like tiny tiger actors,
Attacking spooky shadows, they are mighty jungle hunters.

Stretching, purring, yawning,
There's a new day dawning.
"Meow, meoww, meowww, we want to go to sleep.
Pur, purr, purrr, we'll make not a peep."

Up the stairs they march, like a quartet of weary soldiers,
Four tired kittens trod with tiny drooping shoulders.

Looking down at the disarray, they smile with delight.
Naughty kittens at midnight have made a frightful sight!

So anyone who's had a cat will certainly not ignore,
The mischief caused by one cat is not as bad as four!

Night, Night

www.ingramcontent.com/pod-product-compliance
Lightning Source LLC
Chambersburg PA
CBHW051251110526
44588CB00025B/2951